The Best of Mary Maxim®

MW01156158

Dreamy Baby Wraps

2

4

8

11

14

16

18

24

26

LEISURE ARTS, INC. • Maumelle, Arkansas

Ribbed Shells Blanket

◼◼◼◻ **INTERMEDIATE**

SHOPPING LIST

Yarn (Worsted Weight)

Mary Maxim Baby Kashmere

[1.75 ounces, 109 yards

(50 grams, 101 meters) per ball]:

☐ Any Color   8 balls

Knitting Needle

32" (80 cm) Circular needle

☐ Size 7 (4.50 mm)

     or size needed for gauge

SIZE INFORMATION

Finished: 28" x 32" [71 x 81.5 cm]

GAUGE INFORMATION

One pattern rep (or one fan) = 4"
[10 cm] and 10 rows to 1.75" [4.5 cm]
using **suggested** needle or any size
needle which will give the correct
stitch gauge.

─ STITCH GUIDE ─

See page 29.

INSTRUCTIONS

Cast on 121 sts.

Row 1: (right side) K5,
*yo, [k1, p1] 7 times, k1, yo, k1; rep
from * to last 4 sts, k4. (135 sts)

Row 2: K5, *p2, [k1, p1] 7 times,
p1, k1; rep from * to last 4 sts, k4.

Row 3: K6, yo, [k1, p1] 7 times, k1, yo,
*k3, yo, [k1, p1] 7 times, k1, yo;
rep from * to last 6 sts, k6. (149 sts)

Row 4: K6, p2, [k1, p1] 7 times, p1,
*k3, p2, [k1, p1] 7 times, p1;
rep from * to last 6 sts, k6.

Row 5: K7, yo, [k1, p1] 7 times, k1, yo,
*k5, yo, [k1, p1] 7 times, k1, yo;
rep from * to last 7 sts, k7. (163 sts)

Row 6: K7, p2, [k1, p1] 7 times, p1,
*k5, p2, [k1, p1] 7 times, p1;
rep from * to last 7 sts, k7.

Row 7: K8, yo, [k1, p▇▇▇▇es, k1, yo,
*k7, yo, [k1, p1] 7 tin▇▇, k1, yo;
rep from * to last 8 sts, k8. (177 sts)

Row 8: K8, p2, [k1, p1] 7 times, p1,
*k7, p2, [k1, p1] 7 times, p1;
rep from * to last 8 sts, k8.

Row 9: K9, [sl 1, k1, psso] 3 times,
sl 1, k2tog, psso, [k2tog] 3 times,
*k9, [sl 1, k1, psso] 3 times,
sl 1, k2tog, psso, [k2tog] 3 times;
rep from * to last 9 sts, k9. (121 sts)

Row 10: K4, p to last 4 sts, k4.
Repeat Rows 1-10 until piece
measures about 31" [78.5 cm], ending
after a Row 10.
Knit 10 Rows. Cast off knitwise.
Weave in all ends.

Lovey Baby Blanket

●■■■▶ EXPERIENCED

SHOPPING LIST

Yarn (Worsted Weight)
Mary Maxim Starlette
[3.5 ounces, 180 yards
(100 grams, 165 meters) per ball]:
☐ Any Color   8 balls

Knitting Needles
36" (90 cm) Circular Needle
☐ Size 8 (5.00 mm)

SIZE INFORMATION
Finished: 34.5" x 43" [87.5 x 109 cm]

GAUGE INFORMATION
18 sts and 24 rows to 4" [10 cm] measured over St st using **suggested** needle or any size needle which will give the correct stitch gauge.

─── STITCH GUIDE ───

C2F   Slip next stitch onto cable needle and hold at front of work, k1 from left needle, then k1 from cable needle.

C2B   Slip next stitch onto cable needle and hold at back of work, k1 from left needle, then k1 from cable needle.

C4F   Slip next 2 stitches onto cable needle and hold at front of work, k2 from left needle, then k2 from cable needle.

C4B   Slip next 2 stitches onto cable needle and leave at back of work, k2 from left needle, then k2 from cable needle.

MK   ([K1, p1] 3 times, k1) all in the next stitch (making 7 stitches from one); now pass the 2nd, 3rd, 4th, 5th, 6th, and 7th stitches on the right needle separately over the last stitch made, completing the knot.

T3F   Slip next 2 stitches onto cable needle and hold at front of work, p1 from left needle, then k2 from cable needle.

T3B   Slip next stitch onto cable needle and hold at back of work, k2 from left needle, then p1 from cable needle.

T2F   Slip next stitch onto cable needle and hold at front of work, p1 from left needle, then k1 from cable needle.

T2B   Slip next stitch onto cable needle and hold at back of work, k1 from left needle, then p1 from cable needle.

INSTRUCTIONS

Cable I: (worked over 12 sts)
Rows 1, 5, 9, and 13: (right side) P2, k8, p2.
Row 2 and all even number rows: K2, p8, k2.
Rows 3 and 15: P2, C4B, C4F, p2.
Rows 7 and 11: P2, C4F, C4B, p2.
Row 16: As Row 2.
Repeat these 16 rows for Cable I.

Box Stitch: (worked over 14 sts)
Row 1: (right side) K2, [p2, k2] 3 times.
Row 2: P2, [k2, p2] 3 times.
Row 3: As Row 2.
Row 4: As Row 1.
Repeat these 4 rows for Box Stitch.

Bobble Cable II: (worked over 18 sts)
Row 1: (right side) P5, k1 tbl, p2, k1 tbl, p3, MK, p5.
Row 2: K5, p1, k3, p1, k2, p1, k5.
Row 3: P2, MK, p2, C2F, p1, k1 tbl, p3, k1 tbl, p5.
Row 4: K5, p1, k3, p1, k1, p1, k3, p1, k2.
Row 5: P2, T3F, p1, C2F, k1 tbl, p1, T3B, p2, MK, p2.
Row 6: K2, p1, k4, p1, k1, p2, k2, p1, k4.
Row 7: P4, T3F, C2F, C2B, p2, T3B, p2.
Row 8: K4, p1, k3, p2, k1, p1, k6.
Row 9: P6, C2F, C2B, p1, T3B, p4.
Row 10: K6, p1, k2, p2, k7.
Row 11: P7, C2F, T3B, p6.

Row 12: K8, p3, k7.

Row 13: P7, T3F, p2, MK, p5.

Row 14: K5, p1, k2, p1, k9.

Row 15: P5, MK, p3, k1 tbl, p2, k1 tbl, p5.

Row 16: K5, p1, k2, p1, k3, p1, k5.

Row 17: P5, k1 tbl, p3, k1 tbl, p1, T2B, p2, MK, p2.

Row 18: K2, p1, k3, p1, k1, p1, k3, p1, k5.

Row 19: P2, MK, p2, T3F, p1, k1 tbl, C2B, p1, T3B, p2.

Row 20: K4, p1, k2, p2, k1, p1, k4, p1, k2.

Row 21: P2, T3F, p2, C2F, C2B, T3B, p4.

Row 22: K6, p1, k1, p2, k3, p1, k4.

Row 23: P4, T3F, p1, C2F, C2B, p6.

Row 24: K7, p2, k2, p1, k6.

Row 25: P6, T3F, C2B, p7.

Row 26: K7, p3, k8.

Row 27: P5, MK, p2, T3B, p7.

Row 28: K9, p1, k2, p1, k5.

Repeat these 28 rows for Bobble Cable II.

Cable III: (worked over 8 sts)

Row 1: (right side) P2, C2F, C2B, p2.

Row 2: K2, p4, k2.

Row 3: P2, C2B, C2F, p2.

Row 4: As Row 2.

Repeat these 4 rows for Cable III.

Heart Cable: (worked over 20 sts)

Row 1: (right side) P8, C4F, p8.

Row 2: K8, p4, k8.

Row 3: P7, T3B, T3F, p7.

Row 4: K7, p2, k2, p2, k7.

Row 5: P6, T3B, p2, T3F, p6.

Row 6: K2, [k4, p2] twice, k6.

Row 7: P5, T3B, p4, T3F, p5.

Row 8: K5, p2, k6, p2, k5.

Row 9: P4, [T3B] twice, [T3F] twice, p4.

Row 10: K4, [p2, k1, p2, k2] twice, k2.

Row 11: P3, [T3B] twice, p2, [T3F] twice, p3.

Row 12: K2, [k1, p2] twice, k4, [p2, k1] twice, k2.

Row 13: P3, k1, T2F, T3F, p2, T3B, T2B, k1, p3.

Row 14: K2, [k1, p1] twice, k1, p2, k2, p2, k1, [p1, k1] twice, k2.

Row 15: P3, k1, p1, T2F, T3F, T3B, T2B, p1, k1, p3.

Row 16: K3, p1, k2, p1, k1, p4, k1, p1, k2, p1, k3.

Row 17: P3, T2F, T2B, p1, C4F, p1, T2F, T2B, p3.

Row 18: K4, C2B, k2, p4, k2, C2F, k4.

Repeat Rows 3-18 for Heart Cable.

Blanket: Cast on 144 sts.

Row 1: (right side) Knit.

Row 2: (inc row) K5, [inc one st in next st knitwise] 4 times, k 62, [inc one st in next st knitwise] twice, k 62, [inc one st in next st] 4 times, k5 - 154 sts.

Row 3: K3, work Row 1 of Cable I over next 12 sts, p1, with yarn at back sl 1 purlwise, p1, work Row 1 of Box Stitch over next 14 sts, p1, with yarn at back sl 1 purlwise, p1, work Row 1 of Bobble Cable II over next 18 sts, p1, with yarn at back sl 1 purlwise, p1, work Row 1 of Cable III over next 8 sts, p1, with yarn at back sl 1 purlwise, p1, work Row 1 of Heart Cable over next 20 sts, p1, with yarn at back sl 1 purlwise, p1, work Row 1 of Cable III over next 8 sts, p1, with yarn at back sl 1 purlwise, p1, work Row 1 of Bobble Cable II over next 18 sts, p1, with yarn at back sl 1 purlwise, p1, work Row 1 of Box Stitch over next 14 sts, p1, with yarn at back sl 1 purlwise, p1, work Row 1 of Cable I over next 12 sts, k3.

Row 4: P3, work Row 2 of Cable I over next 12 sts, k1, p1, k1, work Row 2 of Box Stitch over next 14 sts,

k1, p1, k1,

work Row 2 of Bobble Cable II over next 18 sts,

k1, p1, k1,

work Row 2 of Cable III over next 8 sts, k1, p1, k1,

work Row 2 of Heart Cable over next 20 sts,

k1, p1, k1,

work Row 2 of Cable III over next 8 sts, k1, p1, k1,

work Row 2 of Bobble Cable II over next 18 sts,

k1, p1, k1,

work Row 2 of Box Stitch over next 14 sts,

k1, p1, k1,

work Row 2 of Cable I over next 12 sts, p3.

Cable patterns are now in place, with sl st pattern between each cable and 3 sts at beg and end set in St st. Now continue to work through each pattern, until blanket measures approximately 38" [96.5 cm] from cast on edge, ending after a Row 18 of Heart Cable.

Next Row: (right side, dec row) K5, [k2tog] 4 times, k 62, [k2tog] twice, k 62, [k2tog] 4 times, k5. (144 sts) Cast off knitwise.

Border: Cast on 10 sts.

Note: If desired, work border using pair of straight needles the same size as used for Blanket.

Row 1: (right side) K3, [yo, k2tog] twice, [yo] twice, k2tog, k1. (11 sts)

Row 2: K3, p1, k2, [yo, k2tog] twice, k1.

Row 3: K3, [yo, k2tog] twice, k1, [yo] twice, k2tog, k1. (12 sts)

Row 4: K3, p1, k3, [yo, k2tog] twice, k1.

Row 5: K3, [yo, k2tog] twice, k2, [yo] twice, k2tog, k1. (13 sts)

Row 6: K3, p1, k4, [yo, k2tog] twice, k1.

Row 7: K3, [yo, k2tog] twice, k6.

Row 8: Cast off 3 sts, one st rem on right needle, k4, [yo, k2tog] twice, k1. (10 sts)

Repeat these 8 rows of pattern until border measures around entire outside edge of blanket, allowing for gathering at each corner so edges will lay flat.

Do not to cast off until border has been sewn in place; this will allow you to adjust the length of the border if required.

Once border is in place as desired, cast off knitwise.

Sew cast off end to cast on end of border, neatly.

Rainbow Entrelac Blanket

▰▰▰▱ **INTERMEDIATE**

SIZE INFORMATION

Finished: 30" x 40" [76 x 101.5 cm]

GAUGE INFORMATION

One base triangle or one rectangle =
3" [7.5 cm] wide from point to point
and 2 rows of rectangles = 4.75"
[12 cm], using **suggested** needle or
any size needle which will give the
correct stitch gauge.

— STITCH GUIDE —

Kf&b   Increase by knitting into front
and back of stitch indicated.

ssk   Slip next 2 stitches knitwise,
one at a time, to right needle, then
insert left needle through fronts of
both stitches and k2tog as usual.

Note: Due to the nature of this yarn,
each blanket will have its own unique
color sequence.

INSTRUCTIONS

To Make: Cast on 100 sts. Do not join
in rnd, but work back and forth on
circular needle.

Base Triangles:

Row 1: (wrong side) P2, turn.

Row 2: K2, turn.

Row 3: P3, turn.

Row 4: K3, turn.

Row 5: P4, turn.

Row 6: K4, turn.

Row 7: P5, turn.

Row 8: K5, turn.

Row 9: P6, turn.

Row 10: K6, turn.

Row 11: P7, turn.

Row 12: K7, turn.

Row 13: P8, turn.

Row 14: K8, turn.

Row 15: P9, turn.

Row 16: K9, turn.

Row 17: P 10, do not turn.

Repeat these 17 rows 9 times more -
10 triangles.

##Right Corner Triangle:

Row 1: (right side) K2, turn.

Row 2: P2, turn.

Row 3: Kf&b in first st, ssk, turn.

Row 4: P3, turn.

Row 5: Kf&b in first st, k1, ssk, turn.

Row 6: P4, turn.

Row 7: Kf&b in first st, k2, ssk, turn.

Row 8: P5, turn.

Row 9: Kf&b in first st, k3, ssk, turn.

Row 10: P6, turn.

Row 11: Kf&b in first st, k4, ssk, turn.

Row 12: P7, turn.

Row 13: Kf&b in first st, k5, ssk, turn.

Row 14: P8, turn.

Row 15: Kf&b in first st, k6, ssk, turn.

Row 16: P9, turn.

Row 17: Kf&b in first st, k7, ssk, do not
turn.

Leave these 10 sts on right needle.

Right Side Rectangles:

**Pick up row: (right side) Pick up
and k 10 sts evenly along edge of next
triangle (or rectangle), turn.

Row 1: (wrong side) P 10, turn.

Row 2: Sl 1 knitwise, k8, ssk (with
last st of rectangle and first st of next
triangle/rectangle), turn.

Rows 3-20: Repeat Rows 1 and 2 nine
times. Do not turn at end of last row.
Repeat from ****** across row -
9 rectangles completed.

Left Corner Triangle:

Pick up row: (right side) Pick up and
k 10 sts evenly along edge of last
triangle or rectangle, turn.

Row 1: (wrong side) P2tog, p8, turn.

Row 2: K9, turn.

Row 3: P2tog, p7, turn.

Row 4: K8, turn.

Row 5: P2tog, p6, turn.

Row 6: K7, turn.

Row 7: P2tog, p5, turn.

Row 8: K6, turn.

Row 9: P2tog, p4, turn.

Row 10: K5, turn.

Row 11: P2tog, p3, turn.

Row 12: K4, turn.

Row 13: P2tog, p2, turn.

Row 14: K3, turn.

Row 15: P2tog, p1, turn.

Row 16: K2, turn.

Row 17: P2tog, do not turn - 1 st rem.#

Wrong Side Rectangles:

Pick up row: (wrong side) Pick up and p9 sts evenly along edge of triangle just worked, turn - 10 sts on right needle.

***Row 1:* K 10, turn.

Row 2: Sl 1 purlwise, p8, p2tog (with last st of rectangle and first st of next triangle/rectangle), turn.

Rows 3-20: Repeat Rows 1 and 2 nine times. Do Not turn at end of last row.

Next Row: (wrong side) Pick up and p 10 sts evenly along edge of next Right Side Rectangle.
Repeat from ** across row - 10 rectangles completed.
Turn.
Repeat from ## 10 times more - 22 rows of rectangles.

Now rep from ## to # once more, thus ending after a Left Corner Triangle with one st on right needle.

End Triangles:

***Pick up row:** (wrong side) Pick up and p9 sts evenly along edge of triangle just worked - 10 sts on right needle, turn.

Row 1: K 10, turn.

Row 2: P2tog, p7, p2tog, turn.

Row 3: Sl 1 knitwise, k8, turn.

Row 4: P2tog, p6, p2tog, turn.

Row 5: Sl 1 knitwise, k7, turn.

Row 6: P2tog, p5, p2tog, turn.

Row 7: Sl 1 knitwise, k6, turn.

Row 8: P2tog, p4, p2tog, turn.

Row 9: Sl 1 knitwise, k5, turn.

Row 10: P2tog, p3, p2tog, turn.

Row 11: Sl 1 knitwise, k4, turn.

Row 12: P2tog, p2, p2tog, turn.

Row 13: Sl 1 knitwise, k3, turn.

Row 14: P2tog, p1, p2tog, turn.

Row 15: Sl 1 knitwise, k2, turn.

Row 16: [P2tog] twice, turn.

Row 17: Sl 1, k1, turn.

Row 18: [P2tog] twice, do not turn but slip 1st st over 2nd st - one st remains on right needle.
Do Not turn.
Repeat from *** across row, picking up sts along edge of next rectangle instead of triangle.
Fasten off last st at end of row.

I-Cord Border: With right side of Throw facing, beg with top edge, pick up 100 sts across tops of End Triangles.

Using other end of needle (would be right needle), cast on 4 sts.

Slip these 4 sts onto the other end of needle holding sts of Throw (would be left needle), and work as follows:
**K3, k2tog tbl (this joins I-Cord and first edge st tog), then slip these 4 sts back to left needle; rep from ** to last st, [k4, slip sts back to left needle] twice, then k3, k2tog tbl (leave these sts on st holder for the moment)#. Do Not break yarn.

Now with right side facing, working along side of blanket, **pick up** 3 sts to every 4 rows (about 166 sts).

Slip 4 sts from st holder onto left needle,
[k4, slip sts back to left needle] twice, then k3, k2tog tbl,
now rep from ** to #.

Repeat on each rem edge of Throw, being sure to have the same number of sts as before.

Sew ends of I-Cord together.

Weave in all ends.

Blocking: Lay blanket out on a flat surface.

Pin blanket out to correct measurement and cover blanket with fairly damp sheet or towel.

Apply pressure to sheet or towel to transfer moisture through to blanket, then leave until sheet or towel are dry.

Remove and leave blanket to dry.

Double Hearts Blanket

Shown on page 13.

■■■■ **EXPERIENCED**

SIZE INFORMATION

Finished: 32" x 40" [81 x 101.5 cm]

GAUGE INFORMATION

7 sts and 11 rows to 2" [5 cm]
measured over Seed st, using
2 strands of yarn and **suggested**
needles or any size needles which
will give the correct stitch gauge

— STITCH GUIDE —

Note: The Seed st portion of blanket
is worked holding one strand of each
color together and knitting or purling
both strands of the st on the needle
as one.

The double-sided blocks (shown
BOLD in pattern) are worked in
double knitting, purling with one
strand of yarn through the first strand
of each stitch on the needle, then
knitting the second strand of the
same stitch with the other yarn.
Markers are used to help keep the
blocks separated from the seed st
borders.

INSTRUCTIONS

To Make: Using one strand of A and
one strand of B together, cast on
115 sts.

Rows 1-16: K1, *p1, k1; rep from * to
end.
These first 16 rows form Seed st.
Now work double hearts into pattern
as follows:

Row 17: K1, [p1, k1] 5 times, *PM,
**[with both strands of yarn in front,
p1 B, with both strands of yarn in
back, k1 A] 15 times,** PM, k1, [p1, k1]
5 times; rep from * 3 times more.

Row 18: K1, [p1, k1] 5 times, *sl M,
**[with both strands of yarn in front,
p1 A, with both strands of yarn in
back, k1 B] 15 times,**
sl M, k1, [p1, k1] 5 times; rep from * 3
times more.

Row 19: K1, [p1, k1] 5 times, *sl M,
**[with both strands of yarn in front,
p1 B, with both strands of yarn in
back, k1 A] 7 times,**
**with both strands of yarn in front,
p1 A, with both strands of yarn in
back, k1 B,**
**[with both strands of yarn in front,
p1 B, with both strands of yarn in
back, k1 A] 7 times,**
sl M, k1, [p1, k1] 5 times; rep from * 3
times more.

Row 20: K1, [p1, k1] 5 times, *sl M,
**[with both strands of yarn in front,
p1 A, with both strands of yarn in
back, k1 B] 6 times,**
**[with both strands of yarn in front,
p1 B, with both strands of yarn in
back, k1 A] 3 times,**
**[with both strands of yarn in front,
p1 A, with both strands of yarn in
back, k1 B] 6 times,**
sl M, k1, [p1, k1] 5 times; rep from * 3
times more.

Row 21: K1, [p1, k1] 5 times, *sl M,
**[with both strands of yarn in front,
p1 B, with both strands of yarn in
back, k1 A] 5 times,**
**[with both strands of yarn in front,
p1 A, with both strands of yarn in
back, k1 B] 5 times,**
**[with both strands of yarn in front,
p1 B, with both strands of yarn in
back, k1 A] 5 times,**
sl M, k1, [p1, k1] 5 times; rep from * 3
times more.

Row 22: K1, [p1, k1] 5 times, *sl M,
**[with both strands of yarn in front,
p1 A, with both strands of yarn in
back, k1 B] 4 times,**
**[with both strands of yarn in front,
p1 B, with both strands of yarn in
back, k1 A] 7 times,**

[with both strands of yarn in front, p1 A, with both strands of yarn in back, k1 B] 4 times,

sl M, k1, [p1, k1] 5 times; rep from * 3 times more.

Row 23: K1, [p1, k1] 5 times, *sl M,

[with both strands of yarn in front, p1 B, with both strands of yarn in back, k1 A] 3 times,

[with both strands of yarn in front, p1 A, with both strands of yarn in back, k1 B] 9 times,

[with both strands of yarn in front, p1 B, with both strands of yarn in back, k1 A] 3 times,

sl M, k1, [p1, k1] 5 times, rep from * 3 times more.

Row 24: K1, [p1, k1] 5 times, *sl M,

[with both strands of yarn in front, p1 A, with both strands of yarn in back, k1 B] twice,

[with both strands of yarn in front, p1 B, with both strands of yarn in back, k1 A] 11 times,

[with both strands of yarn in front, p1 A, with both strands of yarn in back, k1 B] twice,

sl M, k1, [p1, k1] 5 times; rep from * 3 times more.

Row 25: K1, [p1, k1] 5 times, *sl M,

with both strands of yarn in front, p1 B, with both strands of yarn in back, k1 A,

[with both strands of yarn in front, p1 A, with both strands of yarn in back, k1 B] 13 times,

with both strands of yarn in front, p1 B, with both strands of yarn in

back, k1 A, sl M, k1, [p1, k1] 5 times; rep from * 3 times more.

Row 26: K1, [p1, k1] 5 times, *sl M,

with both strands of yarn in front, p1 A, with both strands of yarn in back, k1 B,

[with both strands of yarn in front, p1 B, with both strands of yarn in back, k1 A] 13 times,

with both strands of yarn in front, p1 A, with both strands of yarn in back, k1 B, sl M,

K1, [p1, k1] 5 times; rep from * 3 times more.

Row 27: Repeat Row 25

Row 28: K1, [p1, k1] 5 times, *sl M,

with both strands of yarn in front, p1 A, with both strands of yarn in back, k1 B,

[with both strands of yarn in front, p1 B, with both strands of yarn in back, k1 A] 6 times,

with both strands of yarn in front, p1 A, with both strands of yarn in back, k1 B,

[with both strands of yarn in front, p1 B, with both strands of yarn in back, k1 A] 6 times,

with both strands of yarn in front, p1 A, with both strands of yarn in back, k1 B, sl M,

K1, [p1, k1] 5 times; rep from * 3 times more.

Row 29: K1, [p1, k1] 5 times, *sl M,

[with both strands of yarn in front, p1 B, with both strands of yarn in back, k1 A] twice,

[with both strands of yarn in front, p1 A, with both strands of yarn in back, k1 B] 4 times,

[with both strands of yarn in front, p1 B, with both strands of yarn in back, k1 A] 3 times,

[with both strands of yarn in front, p1 A, with both strands of yarn in back, k1 B] 4 times,

[with both strands of yarn in front, p1 B, with both strands of yarn in back, k1 A] twice, sl M,

K1, [p1, k1] 5 times; rep from * 3 times more.

Row 30: K1, [p1, k1] 5 times, *sl M,

[with both strands of yarn in front, p1 A, with both strands of yarn in back, k1 B] 3 times,

[with both strands of yarn in front, p1 B, with both strands of yarn in back, k1 A] twice,

[with both strands of yarn in front, p1 A, with both strands of yarn in back, k1 B] 5 times,

[with both strands of yarn in front, p1 B, with both strands of yarn in back, k1 A] twice,

[with both strands of yarn in front, p1 A, with both strands of yarn in back, k1 B] 3 times,

sl M, K1, [p1, k1] 5 times; rep from * 3 times more.

Row 31: Repeat Row 17.
Row 32: Repeat Row 18.
Row 33: Repeat Row 17.
Row 34: Repeat Row 18.

Now rep these 34 rows 5 times more (6 rows of blocks total), then rep Rows 1-16 once.

Cast off in pattern.

Weave in all ends.

Garter & Slip Stitch Blanket

SHOPPING LIST

Yarn (Dk/Sport Weight)

Mary Maxim Baby's Best

[1.75 ounces, 171 yards

(50 grams, 158 meters) per ball]:

☐ White (MC)　　5 balls

☐ Blue or Pink (CC)　　3 balls

Knitting Needle

32" (80 cm) Circular Needle

☐ Size 6 (4.00 mm)
or size needed for gauge

SIZE INFORMATION

Finished: 32" x 34" [81 x 86.5 cm]

GAUGE INFORMATION

22 sts and 40 rows (20 ridges) to 4"
[10 cm] measured over Garter stitch
using **suggested** needle or any size
needle which will give the correct
stitch gauge.

── STITCH GUIDE ──

Note: Body of blanket is worked first,
then borders are added on.
When working body of blanket,
carry color not in use up the side of
work, do not cut yarn with each color
change.
All sts are slipped purlwise.

INSTRUCTIONS

Using MC, cast on 175 sts.

Row 1: (right side) Knit.

Row 2: Purl.

Row 3: Using CC, k2, *sl 1, k1, sl 1, k4;
rep from * to last 5 sts, sl 1, k1, sl 1, k2.

Row 4: K2, *yf, sl 1, yb, k1, yf, sl 1, yb,
k4; rep from * to last 5 sts, yf, sl 1, yb,
k1, yf, sl 1, yb, k2.

Change to MC for next row.

Repeat Rows 1-4 until work measures
about 30" [76 cm] from cast on edge,
ending after a Row 1.

Next Row: Using MC, purl, dec 20 sts
evenly across. (155 sts)

Now continue in pattern as follows:

Top Border:

Row 1: Using MC, kfb, k to last st, kfb.
(157 sts)

Row 2: Knit.

Row 3: As Row 1. (159 sts)

Row 4: Knit.

Row 5: Using CC, rep Row 1. (161 sts)

Row 6: Knit.

Row 7: As Row 1. (163 sts)

Row 8: Knit.

Row 9: Using MC, rep Row 1. (165 sts)

Row 10: Knit.

Row 11: As Row 1. (167 sts)

Row 12: Knit.

Cast off knitwise.

Bottom Border:

Using MC, with right side of blanket
facing, pick up and k 175 sts across
cast on edge of blanket.

Next Row: Purl, dec 20 sts evenly
across. (155 sts).

Repeat Rows 1-12 of Top Border.
Cast off knitwise.

Side Borders:

With right side facing of Blanket
facing, using MC and omitting Top or
Bottom Borders, pick up and k 176 sts
evenly along side of blanket.

Next Row: Purl, dec 20 sts evenly
across. (156 sts)

Now rep Rows 1-12 of Top Border,
having 1 less st for the st count on
each row.

Cast off knitwise.

Repeat on second side of blanket.

Neatly sew edges of borders together
at each corner.

Weave in all ends.

Striped Cables Blanket

■■■□ INTERMEDIATE

SIZE INFORMATION

Finished: 32.5" x 42" [82.5 x 106.5 cm]

GAUGE INFORMATION

One panel measures 6.5" [16.5 cm] wide and 24 rows measures 3.5" [9 cm], using the **suggested** needles or any size needles which will give the correct stitch gauge.

— STITCH GUIDE —

C8B   Slip next 4 sts onto cable needle and hold to back of work, k4 from left-hand needle, then k4 from cable needle.

INSTRUCTIONS

Panel: (make 5, one in each color)
Using Color 1, cast on 38 sts and knit 7 rows.

Next Row: K6, [knit into front and back of next st] 4 times, k 18, [knit into front and back of next st] 4 times, k6 - 46 sts.

Now work in pattern as follows:

Row 1: (right side) K4, p2, k8, p2, k2tog, k5, yo, k2tog, yo, k1, yo, k2, sl 1, k1, psso,
p2, k8, p2, k4.

Row 2: K6, p8, k2, p 14, k2, p8, k6.

Row 3: K4, p2, k8, p2, k2tog, k4, yo, k2tog, yo, k3, yo, k1, sl 1, k1, psso,
p2, k8, p2, k4.

Row 4: Work as Row 2.

Row 5: K4, p2, C8B, p2, k2tog, k3, yo, k2tog, yo, k5, yo, sl 1, k1, psso,
p2, C8B, p2, k4.

Row 6: Work as Row 2.

Row 7: K4, p2, k8, p2, k2tog, k2, yo, k1, yo, sl 1, k1, psso, yo, k5, sl 1, k1, psso,
p2, k8, p2, k4.

Row 8: Work as Row 2.

Row 9: K4, p2, k8, p2, k2tog, k1, yo, k3, yo, sl 1, k1, psso, yo, k4, sl 1, k1, psso,
p2, k8, p2, k4.

Row 10: Work as Row 2.

Row 11: K4, p2, k8, p2, k2tog, yo, k5, yo, sl 1, k1, psso, yo, k3, sl 1, k1, psso,
p2, k8, p2, k4.

Row 12: Work as Row 2.

Repeat these 12 rows of pattern 21 times more, then rep Rows 1-7 once more.

Next Row: K6, [k2tog] 4 times, k 18, [k2tog] 4 times, k6 - 38 sts.
Knit 7 rows. Cast off knitwise.
Repeat using other 4 colors.

To Assemble: Sew panels together neatly in order of color as listed in Shopping List.

Cables Go Round Blanket

 **INTERMEDIATE**

SHOPPING LIST

Yarn (Worsted Weight) [4 MEDIUM]

Mary Maxim Baby Kashmere

[1.75 oz, 109 yards]

(50 grams, 100 meters) per ball]:

☐ Blue   12 balls

Knitting Needles

Double Point Needles (DPN)

☐ Size 8 (5.00 mm)

16" [40 cm] Circular Needle

☐ Size 8 (5.00 mm)

24" [60 cm] Circular Needle

☐ Size 8 (5.00 mm)

36" [90 cm] Circular Needle

☐ Size 8 (5.00 mm)

or size needed for gauge

SIZE INFORMATION

Finished: 41" [104 cm] diameter

GAUGE INFORMATION

Rnds 1-12 = 3.5" [9 cm] diameter and over the larger areas of the blanket, 9 sts and 15 rnds to 2" [5 cm] measured over Seed st and 10 sts and 14 rnds to 2" [5 cm], measured over Twisted Rib all using **suggested** needle or any size needle which will give the correct gauges.

STITCH GUIDE

M3   (K1, p1, k1) all in same stitch.

M1   With left needle, lift horizontal strand of yarn lying between stitch just worked and next stitch, from front to back and knit into the back of the resulting loop.

T5R   Slip next 3 stitches onto cable needle and hold at back of work, k2 from left needle, then p1, k2 from cable needle.

T3B   Slip next stitch onto cable needle and hold at back of work, k2 from left needle, then p1 from cable needle.

T3F   Slip next 2 stitches onto cable needle and hold at front of work, p1 from left needle, then k2 from cable needle.

C3F   Slip next 2 stitches onto cable needle and hold at front of work, k1 from left needle, then k2 from cable needle.

C3B   Slip next stitch onto cable needle and hold at back of work, k2 from left needle, then k1 from cable needle.

K1tbl   Knit 1 through back loop.

T5L   Slip next 2 stitches onto cable needle and hold at front of work, k2, p1 from left needle, then k2 from cable needle.

M1P   With left needle, lift horizontal strand of yarn laying between stitch just worked and next stitch, from back to front and purl as usual into the resulting loop.

Note: Work will begin on 4 DPN's. As sts increase, when you feel you need to, switch to the shortest circular needle and finally to the larger circular needles. Remember once you are working on a circular needle, PM at the beg of the round.

INSTRUCTIONS

Working Circular Cast On (see pg. 23), cast on 8 sts (2 sts on each of 4 DPN).

Rnd 1: Knit, taking care not to twist sts. At this point you might want to use a safety pin to indicate beg of rnds, as a marker is apt to slip off needle.

Rnd 2: (inc rnd) Kf&b of each st. (16 sts)

Rnds 3 and 5: Knit.

Rnd 4: *K1, p1; rep from * around.

Rnd 6: (inc rnd) As Rnd 2. (32 sts)

Rnds 7, 9, 11 and 13: Knit.

Rnds 8, 10 and 12: As Rnd 4.

Rnd 14: (inc rnd) *M3, p1; rep from * around. (64 sts)

Rnds 15 and 17: Knit.

Rnds 16 and 18: *K3, p1; rep from * around.

Rnd 19: (inc rnd) *Slip 1 st onto cable needle and hold behind work, knit next 2 sts, M3 off cable needle, k1; rep from * around. (96 sts)

Rnds 20, 22 and 24: K2, *p1, k5; rep from * to last 4 sts, p1, k3.

Rnds 21 and 23: *K5, p1; rep from * around.

Rnd 25: (inc rnd) *K5, M1, p1, M1; rep from * around. (128 sts)

Rnd 26: *T5R, p1, k1, p1; rep from * around.

Rnd 27: K6, p1, *k7, p1; rep from * to last st, k1.

Rnd 28: *[K2, p1] twice, k1, p1; rep from * around.

Rnd 29: (inc rnd) K2, M1, k1, M1, k3, p1, *k3, M1, k1, M1, k3, p1; rep from * to last st, k1. (160 sts)

Rnds 30 and 32: *K2, p3, k2, p1, k1, p1; rep from * around.

Rnds 31 and 33: K8, p1, *k9, p1; rep from * to last st, k1.

Rnd 34: (inc rnd) *K2, p3, k2, M1, p1, k1, p1, M1; rep from * around. (192 sts)

Rnd 35: *K7, [p1, k1] twice, p1; rep from * around.

At beg of next rnd, reposition marker as instructed.

Rnd 36: Remove M, slip first 2 sts onto cable needle and hold in front of work, slip next st purlwise to right-hand needle (it will be worked at end of rnd), PM and k2 sts from cable needle, p1, T3B, [k1, p1] twice, k1, *T3F, p1, T3B, [k1, p1] twice, k1; rep from * to last st, p1.

Rnd 37: *T5R, [k1, p1] 3 times, k1; rep from * around.

Rnd 38: (inc rnd) *K2, p1, k2, M1, [p1, k1] 3 times, p1, M1; rep from * around. (224 sts)

Rnd 39: *K2, p1, k2, [p1, k1] 4 times, p1; rep from * around.

Rnd 40: K2, p1, k3, [p1, k1] 3 times, p1, *k3, p1, k3, [p1, k1] 3 times, p1; rep from * to last st, k1.

Rnd 41: *T5R, [p1, k1] 4 times, p1; rep from * around.

Reposition marker again in each of the next three rows as follows:

Rnd 42: Remove M, slip first 3 sts purlwise to right-hand needle and leave unworked, PM (marker has shifted 3 sts to the left), *C3F, [p1, k1] 3 times, p1, C3B, k1; rep from * around.

Rnd 43: Remove M, slip first st purlwise to right-hand needle and leave unworked, PM (marker has shifted 1 st to the left), *K3, [p1, k1] twice, p1, k3, p3; rep from * around.

Rnd 44: **Remove M, slip first 2 sts onto cable needle and hold in front of work, slip next st purlwise to right-hand needle and leave unworked, PM, then k2 from cable needle**, [k1, p1] twice, k1, C3B, *k3, C3F, [k1, p1] twice, k1, C3B; rep from * to last 4 sts, k4.

Rnd 45: *K2, [p1, k1] twice, p1, k2, p5; rep from * around.

Continue to reposition marker as in Rnd 44, on the next and then the following alternate rnd.

Rnd 46: Work first 3 sts as for Rnd 44 from ** to **, p1, k1, p1, C3B, k5, *C3F, p1, k1, p1, C3B, k5; rep from * to last st, k1.

Rnd 47: *K3, p1, k3, p7; rep from * around.

Rnd 48: Work first 3 sts as for Rnd 44 from ** to **, k1, C3B, k7, *C3F, k1, C3B, k7; rep from * to last st, k1.

Rnd 49: *K2, p1, k2, p9; rep from * around.

Rnd 50: *T5L, k9; rep from * around.

Rnd 51: As Rnd 49.

Rnd 52: (inc rnd) *K2, p1, k2, M1, k9, M1; rep from * around. (256 sts)

Rnd 53: *K2, p1, k2, p 11; rep from * around.

Rnd 54: *T5L, k 11; rep from * around.

Rnd 55: As Rnd 53.

Rnd 56: K2, p1, *k 15, p1; rep from * to last 13 sts, k 13.

Rnd 57: As Rnd 53.

Rnd 58: As Rnd 54.

Rnd 59: As Rnd 53.

Rnd 60: As Rnd 56.

Once again, marker is on the move!

Rnd 61: Remove M, slip first 3 sts purlwise to right-hand needle and leave unworked, PM (marker has shifted 3 sts to the left), *k2, p 11, k2, p1; rep from * around.

Rnd 62: (inc rnd) *K 15, M1, p1, M1; rep from * around. (288 sts)

Continue to reposition marker, as in Rnd 44, on the next and then every alternate rnd, 4 times more.

Rnd 63: Work first 3 sts as for Rnd 44 from ** to **, p9, T3B, k1tbl, p1, k1tbl, *T3F, p9, T3B, k1tbl, p1, k1tbl; rep from * to last st, p1.

Rnd 64: *K 13, [p1, k1tbl] twice, p1; rep from * around.

Rnd 65: Work first 3 sts as for Rnd 44 from ** to **, p7, C3B, [p1, k1tbl] twice, p1, *C3F, p7, C3B, [p1, k1tbl] twice, p1; rep from * to last st, k1.

Rnd 66: *K 11, [k1tbl, p1] 3 times, k1tbl; rep from * around.

Rnd 67: Work first 3 sts as for Rnd 44 from ** to **, p5, T3B, [k1tbl, p1] 3 times, k1tbl, *T3F, p5, T3B, [k1tbl, p1] 3 times, k1tbl; rep from * to last st, p1.

Rnd 68: *K9, [p1, k1tbl] 4 times, p1; rep from * around.

Rnd 69: Work first 3 sts as for Rnd 44 from ** to **, p3, C3B, [p1, k1tbl] 4 times, p1, *C3F, p3, C3B, [p1, k1tbl] 4 times, p1; rep from * to last st, k1.

Rnd 70: *K7, [k1tbl, p1] 5 times, k1tbl; rep from * around.

Rnd 71: Work first 3 sts as for Rnd 44 from ** to **, p1, T3B, [k1tbl, p1] 5 times, k1tbl, *T3F, p1, T3B, [k1tbl, p1] 5 times, k1tbl; rep from * to last st, p1.

Rnd 72: (inc rnd) K5, M1, [p1, k1tbl] 6 times, p1, M1; rep from * around. (320 sts)

Rnd 73: *T5R, *[k1tbl, p1] 7 times, k1tbl* for Twisted Rib; rep from * around.

Rnd 74: *K5, work Twisted Rib as established over next 15 sts; rep from * around.

Rnd 75: *K2, p1, k2, work Twisted Rib as established over next 15 sts; rep from * to end.

Rnd 76: As Rnd 74.

Rnd 77: As Rnd 73.

Rnd 78: As Rnd 74.

Rnd 79: As Rnd 75.

After this rnd, the word "Rib" is used for the Twisted Rib and later "Seed" for Seed St.

Rnd 80: (inc rnd) *K2, M1, k1, M1, k2, Rib next 15 sts; rep from * around. (352 sts)

Rnds 81, 83 and 85: *K2, p3, k2, Rib next 15 sts; rep from * around.

Rnds 82, 84 and 86: *K7, Rib next 15 sts; rep from * around.

Once again, marker is on the move.

Rnd 87: Work first 3 sts as for Rnd 44 from ** to **, p1, T3B, Rib next 15 sts, *T3F, p1, T3B, Rib next 15 sts; rep from * to last st, p1.

Rnd 88: (inc rnd) *T5R, M1, [p1, k1tbl] 8 times, p1, M1; rep from * around. (384 sts)

Rnds 89, 90 and 91: K2, p1, k2, Rib next 19 sts; rep from * around.

Rnd 92: *T5R, Rib next 19 sts; rep from * around.

Again, marker has to be moved.

Rnd 93: Remove M, slip first 3 sts purlwise to right-hand needle and leave unworked, PM (maker has shifted 3 sts to the left), T3F, [p1, k1tbl] 8 times, p1, *T3B, k1, T3F, [p1, k1tbl] 8 times, p1; rep from * to last 4 sts, T3B, k1.

Rnd 94: Remove M, slip 1 st purlwise to right-hand needle and leave unworked, PM, k2, Rib next 17 sts, *k3, p1, k3, Rib next 17 sts; rep from * to last 5 sts, k3, p1, k1.

Continue to reposition marker, as in Rnd 44, on the next and then every alternate round 7 times more.

Rnd 95: Work first 3 sts as for Rnd 44 from ** to **, Rib next 15 sts, *C3B, p1, k1, p1, C3F, Rib next 15 sts; rep from * to last 7 sts, C3B, [p1, k1] twice.

Rnd 96: (inc rnd) *K2, Rib next 15 sts, k2, M1, [p1, k1] twice, p1, M1; rep from * around. (416 sts)

Rnd 97: Work first 3 sts as for Rnd 44 from ** to **, Rib 13, C3B, [p1, k1] 3 times, p1; *C3F, Rib 13, C3B, [p1, k1] 3 times, p1; rep from * to last st, k1.

Rnd 98: *K2, Rib 13, k2, work in Seed St as established over next 9 sts; rep from * around.

Rnd 99: Work first 3 sts as for Rnd 44 from ** to **, Rib 11, T3B, Seed St as established over next 9 sts, *T3F, Rib 11, T3B, Seed St next 9, rep from * to last st, p1.

Rnd 100: *K2, Rib 11, k2, Seed 11; rep from * around.

Rnd 101: Work first 3 sts as for Rnd 44 from ** to **, Rib 9, C3B, Seed 11, *C3F, Rib 9, C3B, Seed 11; rep from * to last st, k1.

Rnd 102: *K2, Rib 9, k2, Seed 13; rep from * around.

Rnd 103: Work first 3 sts as for Rnd 44 from ** to **, Rib 7, T3B, Seed 13, *T3F, Rib 7, T3B, Seed 13; rep from * to last st, p1.

Rnd 104: (inc rnd) *K2, Rib 7, k2, M1P, [k1, p1] 7 times, k1, M1P; rep from * around. (448 sts)

Rnd 105: Work first 3 sts as for Rnd 44 from ** to **, Rib 5, T3B, Seed 17, *T3F, Rib 5, T3B, Seed 17; rep from * to last st, p1.

Rnd 106: *K2, Rib 5, k2, Seed 19; rep from * around.

Rnd 107: Work first 3 sts as for Rnd 44 from ** to **, Rib 3, C3B, Seed 19, *C3F, Rib 3, C3B, Seed 19; rep from * to last st, k1.

Rnd 108: *K2, Rib 3, k2, Seed 21; rep from * around.

Rnd 109: Work first 3 sts as for Rnd 44 from ** to **, p1, T3B, Seed 21, *T3F, p1, T3B, Seed 21; rep from * to last st, p1.

Rnd 110: *K2, p1, k2, Seed 23; rep from * around.

Rnd 111: *T5L, Seed 23, rep from * around.

Rnds 112 and 114: K2, p1, k3, Seed 21, *k3, p1, k3, Seed 21; rep from * to last st, k1.

Rnd 113: *K2, p1, k2, Seed 23; rep from * around.

Rnd 115: (inc rnd) *T5L, M1, [p1, k1] 11 times, p1, M1; rep from * around. (480 sts)

Again, marker needs to move.

Rnd 116: Remove M, slip 3 sts purlwise to right-hand needle and leave unworked, PM, k2, Seed 25, *k5, Seed 25; rep from * to last 3 sts, k3.

Rnd 117: *K3, Seed 23, k3, p1; rep from * around.

Rnd 118: (inc rnd) *K2, Seed 25, k2, M1, k1, M1; rep from * around. (512 sts)

Rnd 119: *K3, Seed 23, k3, p3: rep from * around.

Continue to reposition marker, as in Rnd 44, on the next and then every alternate round 11 times more.

Rnd 120: Work first 3 sts as for Rnd 44 from ** to **, Seed 23, C3B, k3, *C3F, Seed 23, C3B, k3; rep from * to last st, k1.

Rnd 121: *K2, Seed 23, k2, p5; rep from * around.

Rnd 122: Work first 3 sts as for Rnd 44 from ** to **, Seed 21, C3B, k5, *C3F, Seed 21, C3B, k5; rep from * to last st, k1.

Rnd 123: *K3, Seed 19, k3, p7; rep from * around.

Rnd 124: Work first 3 sts as for Rnd 44 from ** to **, Seed 19, C3B, k7, *C3F, Seed 19, C3B, k7; rep from * to last st, k1.

Rnd 125: *K2, Seed 19, k2, p9; rep from * around.

Rnd 126: (inc rnd) Work first 3 sts as for Rnd 44 from ** to **, Seed 17, C3B, M1, k9, M1, *C3F, Seed 17, C3B, M1, k9, M1; rep from * to last st, k1. (544 sts)

Rnd 127: *K3, Seed 15, k3, p 13; rep from * around.

Rnd 128: Work first 3 sts as for Rnd 44 from ** to **, Seed 15, C3B, k 13, *C3F, Seed 15, C3B, k 13; rep from * to last st, k1.

Rnd 129: *K2, Seed 15, k2, p 15; rep from * around.

Rnd 130: Work first 3 sts as for Rnd 44 from ** to **, Seed 13, C3B, k 15, *C3F, Seed 13, C3B, k 15; rep from * to last st, k1.

Rnd 131: *K3, Seed 11, k3, p 17; rep from * around.

Rnd 132: Work first 3 sts as for Rnd 44 from ** to **, Seed 11, C3B, k 17, *C3F, Seed 11, C3B, k 17; rep from * to last st, k1.

Rnd 133: *K2, Seed 11, k2, p 19; rep from * around.

Rnd 134: (inc rnd) Work first 3 sts as for Rnd 44 from ** to **, Seed 9, C3B, M1, k 19, M1, *C3F, Seed 9, C3B, M1, k 19, M1; rep from * to last st, k1. (576 sts)

Rnd 135: *K3, Seed 7, k3, p 23; rep from * around.

Rnd 136: Work first 3 sts as for Rnd 44 from ** to **, Seed 7, C3B, k 23, *C3F, Seed 7, C3B, k 23; rep from * to last st k1.

Rnd 137: *K2, Seed 7, k2, p 25; rep from * around.

Rnd 138: Work first 3 sts as for Rnd 44 from ** to **, Seed 5, C3B, k 25, *C3F, Seed 5, C3B, k 25; rep from * to last st, k1.

Rnd 139: *K3, Seed 3, k3, p 27; rep from * around.

Rnd 140: Work first 3 sts as for Rnd 44 from ** to **, Seed 3, C3B, k 27, *C3F, Seed 3, C3B, k 27; rep from * to last st, k1.

Rnd 141: *K2, Seed 3, k2, p 29; rep from * around.

Rnd 142: Work first 3 sts as for Rnd 44 from ** to **, p1, C3B, k 29, *C3F, p1, C3B, k 29; rep from * to last st, k1.

Rnd 143: (inc rnd) K1tbl, M1P, k1tbl, p1, [k1tbl, M1P] twice, p 31, *[M1P, k1tbl] twice, p1, [k1tbl, M1P] twice, p 31; rep from * around, M1P. (640 sts)

Rnd 144: [K1tbl, p1] 4 times, k 31, *p1, [k1tbl, p1] 4 times, k 31; rep from * to last st, p1.

Rnd 145: *Rib 7, p 33; rep from * around.

Rnd 146: As Rnd 144.

Rnd 147: Work sts as Rnd 145 AND AT THE SAME TIME, cast off loosely in pattern.

Weave in all ends.

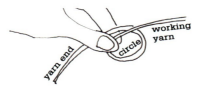

Circular Cast On: To begin, create a circle using the end of the yarn. Pinch the circle in your left hand, and hold the needle and working yarn in your right hand.
You will create new sts using the point of the needle, working into the center of the circle.

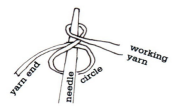

1. Insert needle into circle from front to back.
2. Wrap yarn around needle.

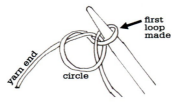

3. Using needle point, pull loop through circle from back to front (1 new loop on needle).

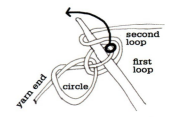

4. Wrap working yarn around needle (2 new loops on needle)
5. Use finger to lift first loop over second loop and off the needle (1 loop remains; this is one st cast on).

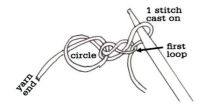

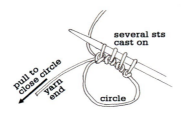

Repeat Steps 1-5 until there are 8 sts cast on.
Divide sts onto DPN's as instructed, then pull tail of yarn to close the circle.

Sweetheart Lace Blanket

◼◼◼◻ INTERMEDIATE

SHOPPING LIST

Yarn (Fingering Weight)
Mary Maxim Twinkle
[1.75 oz, 230 yards]
(50 grams, 210 meters) per ball]:
☐ Pink 7 balls

Knitting Needle
☐ Size 3 (3.25 mm)
or size needed for gauge

SIZE INFORMATION
Finished: 33" x 36" [84 x 91.5 cm]

GAUGE INFORMATION
Widest part of "leaf" = 2.25" [5.5 cm]
and one rep of 24 rows to 2.25"
[5.5 cm], measured over pattern
using **suggested** needles or
any size needles which will give
the correct stitch gauge.

── STITCH GUIDE ──
SKP Slip next stitch, knit 1, pass
slipped stitch over.

INSTRUCTIONS
To Make: Cast on 241 sts.
Row 1: (right side) K1, yo, SKP, k7,
*k8, k2tog, yo, k1, yo, SKP, k7;
rep from * to last 11 sts, k8, k2tog, yo,
k1.

Row 2: Purl.
Row 3: K2, yo, SKP, k6,
*k7, k2tog, yo, k3, yo, SKP, k6;
rep from * to last 11 sts, k7, k2tog, yo,
k2.
Row 4: Purl.
Row 5: K3, yo, SKP, k5,
*k6, k2tog, yo, k5, yo, SKP, k5;
rep from * to last 11 sts, k6, k2tog, yo,
k3.
Row 6: Purl.
Row 7: K4, yo, SKP, k4,
*k5, k2tog, yo, k7, yo, SKP, k4;
rep from * to last 11 sts, k5, k2tog, yo,
k4.
Row 8: P1, yo, p4, p2tog, p4,
*p3, p2tog tbl, p4, yo, p1, yo, p4,
p2tog, p4;
rep from * to last 10 sts, p3, p2tog tbl,
p4, yo, p1.
Row 9: K2, yo, k4, SKP, k2,
*k3, k2tog, k4, yo, k3, yo, k4, SKP, k2;
rep from * to last 11 sts, k3, k2tog, k4,
yo, k2.
Row 10: P3, yo, p4, p2tog, p2,
*p1, p2tog tbl, p4, yo, p5, yo, p4,
p2tog, p2;
rep from * to last 10 sts, p1, p2tog tbl,
p4, yo, p3.
Row 11: K4, yo, k4, SKP,
*k1, k2tog, k4, yo, k7, yo, k4, SKP;
rep from * to last 11 sts, k1, k2tog, k4,
yo, k4.
Row 12: Purl.
Row 13: K8, k2tog, yo,
*k1, yo, SKP, k 15, k2tog, yo;

rep from * to last 11 sts, k1, yo, SKP,
k8.
Row 14: Purl.
Row 15: K7, k2tog, yo, k1,
*k2, yo, SKP, k 13, k2tog, yo, k1;
rep from * to last 11 sts, k2, yo, SKP,
k7.
Row 16: Purl.
Row 17: K6, k2tog, yo, k2,
*k3, yo, SKP, k 11, k2tog, yo, k2;
rep from * to last 11 sts, k3, yo, SKP,
k6.
Row 18: Purl.
Row 19: K5, k2tog, yo, k3,
*k4, yo, SKP, k9, k2tog, yo, k3;
rep from * to last 11 sts, k4, yo, SKP,
k5.
Row 20: P4, p2tog tbl, p4, yo, p1,
*yo, p4, p2tog, p7, p2tog tbl, p4, yo,
p1; rep from * to last 10 sts, yo, p4,
p2tog, p4.
Row 21: K3, k2tog, k4, yo, k1,
*k2, yo, k4, SKP, k5, k2tog, k4, yo, k1;
rep from * to last 11 sts, k2, yo, k4,
SKP, k3.
Row 22: P2, p2tog tbl, p4, yo, p3,
*p2, yo, p4, p2tog, p3, p2tog tbl, p4,
yo, p3; rep from * to last 10 sts, p2, yo,
p4, p2tog, p2.
Row 23: K1, k2tog, k4, yo, k3,
*k4, yo, k4, SKP, k1, k2tog, k4, yo, k3;
rep from * to last 11 sts, k4, yo, k4,
SKP, k1.
Row 24: Purl.

Repeat these 24 rows of pattern until piece measures about 31" [78.5 cm] from cast on edge, ending after a Row 24. Cast off.

Lace Border: Cast on 7 sts.
Row 1: (right side) K3, yo, SKP, yo, k2. (8 sts)
Rows 2, 4, 6, 8, 10, 12, 14: Slip 1 purlwise, p to last 2 sts, k2.
Row 3: K4, yo, SKP, yo, k2. (9 sts)
Row 5: K5, yo, SKP, yo, k2. (10 sts)

Row 7: K6, yo, SKP, yo, k2. (11 sts)
Row 9: K7, yo, SKP, yo, k2. (12 sts)
Row 11: K8, yo, SKP, yo, k2. (13 sts)
Row 13: K9, yo, SKP, yo, k2. (14 sts)
Row 15: K 10, yo, SKP, yo, k2. (15 sts)
Row 16: Cast off 8 sts, p4, k2. (7 sts)
Repeat these 16 rows of pattern until piece measures long enough to sew around entire outside edge of blanket, allowing extra to gather at each corner, with outside edge lying flat.

When border is long enough, end after a Row 16. Leave rem sts on needle so that the border can be adjusted in length if needed once it is sewn in place.
Sew border in place, gathering in each corner as desired, then cast off rem sts.
Sew cast on edge to cast off edge neatly.

25

Little Blossoms Baby Blanket

SHOPPING LIST

Yarn (Dk/Sport Weight)

Mary Maxim Baby's Best
[1.75 ounces, 171 yards
(50 grams, 158 meters) per ball]:

☐ Mint   8 balls

Knitting Needle
32" (80 cm) Circular Needle

☐ Size 7 (4.50 mm)
or size needed for gauge

SIZE INFORMATION
Finished: 32" x 38" [81 x 96.5 cm]

GAUGE INFORMATION
Side Panels measure 6.5" [16.5 cm],
Center Panel measures 19" [48 cm]
over pattern using **suggested** needle
or any size needle which will give the
correct stitch gauge.

── STITCH GUIDE ──

C2B   Knit into front of 2nd st on left
needle, then knit into back of first st
of left needle, slipping both sts off left
needle at the same time - 2 sts now on
right needle, with the 2nd st sitting in
front of the first st.

SKP   slip one stitch, knit one stitch,
pass slipped stitch over knit stitch.

KPK   (K1, p1, k1) all in next stitch.

Note: If desired, place a marker
between each pattern. It will be easier
to find mistakes as you work; or, if you
were to get interrupted you will be
able to find where you left off.

────────────

INSTRUCTIONS

To Make: Cast on 182 sts. Do Not join
in rnd, but work back and forth in
Seed st as follows:

Row 1: (right side) *K1, p1; rep from *
across.

Row 2: *P1, k1; rep from * across.
Repeat these last 2 rows 3 more
times.

Now set patterns as follows:
Now keeping the first 8 sts and last
8 sts in Seed st as set, work Side and
Center Panels as follows:

Row 1: (right side) K2, [p 12, k2] twice,
k1, PM (these 31 sts form side panel),
p4, [k1, p4, yo, k1, yrn, p4] 10 times,
PM,
(these center sts form center panel),
k3, [p 12, k2] twice, PM (these last 31
sts form other side panel) - 202 sts.

Row 2: P2, *[KPK all in one st, p3tog] 3
times, p2, rep from * once more, k1,
sl M, k4, [yrn, p3, yo, k4, p1, k4] 10
times, sl M,
k1, p2, **[KPK in next st, p3tog] 3
times, p2, rep from ** once more - 222
sts.

Row 3: K2, [p 12, k2] twice, k1, sl M,
p4, [k1, p4, yo, k5, yrn, p4] 10 times,
sl M,

k3, [p 12, k2] twice - 242 sts.

Row 4: P2, *[p3tog, KPK in next st] 3
times, p2, rep from * once more, k1,
sl M,
k4, [yrn, p7, yrn, k4, p1, k4] 10 times,
sl M,
k1, p2, **[p3tog, KPK in next st] 3
times, p2, rep from ** once more -
262 sts.

Row 5: C2B, [p 12, C2B] twice, k1, sl M,
p4, [k1, p4, yo, k9, yrn, p4] 10 times,
sl M,
k1, C2B, [p 12, C2B] twice - 282 sts.

Row 6: P2, *[KPK all in one st, p3tog]
3 times, p2, rep from * once more, k1,
sl M,
k4, [p2tog, p7, p2tog tbl, k4, p1, k4] 10
times, sl M,
k1, p2, **[KPK in next st, p3tog] 3
times, p2, rep from ** once more -
262 sts.

Row 7: K2, [p 12, k2] twice, k1, sl M,
p4, [k1, p4, SKP, k5, k2tog, p4] 10
times, sl M,
k3, [p 12, k2] twice - 242 sts.

Row 8: P2, *[p3tog, KPK in next st] 3
times, p2, rep from * once more, k1,
sl M,
k4, [p2tog, p3, p2tog tbl, k4, p1, k4] 10
times, sl M,
k1, p2, **[p3tog, KPK in next st] 3
times, p2; rep from ** once more -
222 sts.

Row 9: C2B, [p 12, C2B] twice, k1, sl M, p4, [k1, p4, SKP, k1, k2tog, p4] 10 times, sl M,
k1, C2B, [p 12, C2B] twice - 202 sts.

Row 10: P2, *[KPK all in one st, p3tog] 3 times, p2, rep from * once more, k1, sl M,
k4, [p3tog, k4, p1, k4] 10 times, sl M, k1, p2, **[KPK in next st, p3tog] 3 times, p2, rep from ** once more - 182 sts.

Row 11: K2, [p 12, k2] twice, k1, sl M, p4, [yo, k1, yrn, p4, k1, p4] 10 times, sl M,
k3, [p 12, k2] twice - 202 sts.

Row 12: P2, *[p3tog, KPK in next st] 3 times, p2, rep from * once more, k1, sl M, k4, [p1, k4, yrn, p3, yo, k4] 10 times, sl M,
k1, p2, **[p3tog, KPK in next st] 3 times, p2; rep from ** once more - 222 sts.

Row 13: C2B, [p 12, C2B] twice, k1, sl M,
p4, [yo, k5, yrn, p4, k1, p4] 10 times, sl M,
k1, C2B, [p 12, C2B] twice - 242 sts.

Row 14: P2, *[KPK all in one st, p3tog] 3 times, p2, rep from * once more, k1, sl M, k4, [p1, k4, yrn, p7, yo, k4] 10 times, sl M,
k1, p2, **[KPK in next st, p3tog] 3 times, p2, rep from ** once more - 262 sts.

Row 15: K2, [p 12, k2] twice, k1, sl M, p4, [yo, k9, yrn, p4, k1, p4] 10 times, sl M,
k3, [p 12, k2] twice - 282 sts.

Row 16: P2, *[p3tog, KPK in next st] 3 times, p2, rep from * once more, k1, sl M,
k4, [p1, k4, p2tog, p7, p2tog tbl, k4] 10 times, sl M,
k1, p2, **[p3tog, KPK in next st] 3 times, p2; rep from ** once more - 262 sts.

Row 17: C2B, [p 12, C2B] twice, k1, sl M, p4, [SKP, k5, k2tog, p4, k1, p4] 10 times, sl M,
k1, C2B, [p 12, C2B] twice - 242 sts.

Row 18: P2, *[KPK all in one st, p3tog] 3 times, p2, rep from * once more, k1, sl M,

k4, [p1, k4, p2tog, p3, p2tog tbl, k4] 10 times, sl M,
k1, p2, **[KPK in next st, p3tog] 3 times, p2, rep from ** once more - 222 sts.

Row 19: K2, [p 12, k2] twice, k1, sl M, p4, [SKP, k1, k2tog, p4, k1, p4] 10 times, sl M,
k3, [p 12, k2] twice - 202 sts.

Row 20: P2, *[p3tog, KPK in next st] 3 times, p2, rep from * once more, k1, sl M,
k4, [p1, k4, p3tog, k4] 10 times, sl M, k1, p2, **[p3tog, KPK in next st] 3 times, p2; rep from ** once more - 182 sts.

Row 21: C2B, [p 12, C2B] twice, k1, sl M, p4, [k1, p4, yo, k1, yrn, p4] 10 times, sl M,
k1, C2B, [p 12, C2B] twice - 202 sts. Now repeat Rows 2-21 ten more times.
Repeat Rows 2-20 once more.
Work in Seed st over all sts until 8 rows have been completed.
Cast off all sts in pattern.

General Instructions

ABBREVIATIONS

"	inches
approx.	approximately
beg	begin or beginning
CC	Contrast Color
cm	centimeter
dec	decrease or decreasing
gm	gram
inc	increase or increasing
K	knit
kfb	knit into front & back of st
P	purl
PM	place marker
psso	pass slipped stitch over
M	marker
MC	Main Color
mm	millimeter
rem	remain or remaining
rep	repeat
rnd	round
sl	slip
st	stitch
sts	stitches
St st	Stocking stitch
tbl	through back loop
tog	together
yb	bring yarn to back of work
yds	yards
yf	bring yarn in front of work
yo	yarn over
yrn	yarn forward and around needle

SYMBOLS & TERMS

* or # work instructions following or between * or # as many more times as indicated in addition to the first time.

() or [ ] work enclosed instructions as many times as specified by the number immediately following **or** work all enclosed instructions in the stitch or space indicated **or** contains explanatory remarks

— the number(s) given after a hyphen at the end of a row or round denote(s) the number of stitches or spaces you should have on that row or round.

KNIT TERMINOLOGY

UNITED STATES		INTERNATIONAL
gauge	=	tension
bind off	=	cast off

Yarn Weight Symbol & Names	1 SUPER FINE	2 FINE	3 LIGHT	4 MEDIUM	5 BULKY	6 SUPER BULKY	7 JUMBO
Type of Yarns in Category	Sock, Fingering Baby	Sport, Baby	DK, Light Worsted	Worsted, Afghan Aran	Chunky, Craft, Rug	Super Bulky, Roving	Jumbo, Roving
Knit Gauge Range in Stockinette St to 4" (10 cm)	27-32 sts	23-26 sts	21-24 sts	16-20 sts	12-15 sts	7-11 sts	6 sts and fewer
Advised Needle Size Range	1 to 3	3 to 5	5 to 7	7 to 9	9 to 11	11 to 17	17 and larger

*GUIDELINES ONLY: The chart above reflects the most commonly used gauges and needle sizes for specific yarn categories.

BEGINNER	Projects for first-time knitters using basic knit and purl stitches. Minimal shaping.
EASY	Projects using basic stitches, repetitve stitch patterns, simple color changes, and simple shaping and finishing.
INTERMEDIATE	Projects with a variety of stitches, such as basic cables and lace, simple intarsia, double-pointed needles and knitting in the round needle techniques, mid-level shaping and finishing.
EXPERIENCED	Projects using advanced techniques and stitches, such as short rows, fair isle, more intricate intarsia, cables, lace patterns and numerous color changes.

KNITTING NEEDLES

U.S.	50	35	19	17	15	13	11	----	----	10.5	10	9	8	7	6	5	4	3	----	2	1	0	----
U.K.	---	----	----	----	000	00	0	1	2	3	4	5	6	7	8	9	----	10	11	12	13	14	15
Metric mm	25	19	15	12.75	10	9	8	7.5	7	6.5	6	5.5	5	4.5	4	3.75	3.5	3.25	3	2.75	2.25	2	1.75

Casting On

1a. Make a slip knot: Loop the yarn as shown and slip needle under the lower strand of the loop.
1b. Pull up a loop of yarn.

2. Pull the yarn end attached to the ball of yarn to tighten the slip knot leaving the other end approx. 4" [10 cm] long. Transfer needle to left hand.

3a. Insert the right-hand needle through slip knot and wind yarn over right-hand needle.
3b. Pull loop through slip knot.

4. Place new loop on left-handle needle. (You now have 2 stitches (sts) on your left-hand needle).

5. Insert right-hand needle between last 2 stitches (sts) on left-hand needle and wind yarn over right-hand needle.

6. Pull loop through. Place this new loop on left-hand needle beside last stitch (st). (You now have 1 more stitch on left-hand needle). Repeat (rep) steps 5 and 6 until required number of stitches (sts) have been cast on left-hand needle.

The Knit Stitch

1. Hold the needle with cast on stitches (sts) in your left hand, and the loose yarn attached to the ball at the back of work. Insert right-hand needle from left to right through the front of the first stitch (st) on the left-hand needle.

2. Wind the yarn from left to right over the point of the right-hand needle.

3. Draw the yarn through this original stitch (st) which forms a new stitch (st) on right-hand needle.

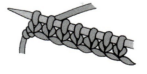

4. Slip the original stitch (st) off the left-hand needle, keeping the new stitch (st) on the right-hand needle.

5. To knit a row, repeat steps 1 to 4 until all stitches (sts) have been transferred from left-hand needle to right-hand needle. Turn the work by transferring the needle with stitches (sts) into your left hand to knit the next row.

The Purl Stitch

1. With yarn at front of work, insert right-hand needle from right to left through front of first stitch (st) on left-hand needle.

2. Wind yarn around right-hand needle. Pull yarn through stitch (st).

3. Slip original stitch (st) off needle. Repeat (rep) these steps until all stitches (sts) on left-hand needle have been transferred onto right-hand needle to complete one row of purling.

Increasing and Decreasing

Increase 1 stitch (st) in next stitch (st): Work into front and back of stitch (st) as follows: Knit stitch (st), then before slipping it off needle, twist right-hand needle behind left-hand needle and knit again into back of loop. Slip original stitch (st) off needle. There are now 2 stitches (sts) on right-hand needle made from original stitch.

K2tog Decrease: Knit 2 stitches (sts) together (tog) through the front of both loops.

P2tog Decrease: Purl 2 stitches (sts) together (tog) through the front of both loops.

Casting Off

Cast off using knit stitch (knitwise): Knit the first 2 stitches (sts). *Using left-hand needle, lift first stitch (st) over second stitch (st) and drop it off between points of the 2 needles. Knit the next stitch (st); repeat (rep) from * until all stitches (sts) from left-hand needle have been worked and only 1 stitch (st) remains on the right-hand needle. Cut yarn (leaving enough to sew in end) and thread cut end through stitch (st) on needle. Draw yarn up firmly to fasten off last stitch (st).

Cast off using purl stitch (purlwise): Purl first 2 stitches (sts). *Using left-hand needle, lift first stitch (st) over second stitch (st) and drop it off needle. Purl next stitch (st) as described for casting off knitwise.

Yarn Information

Projects in this book were made with different weight yarns. Any brand of yarn may be used.
It is best to refer to yardage/meters when determining how many balls or skeins to purchase.
Remember, to arrive at the finished size, it is the GAUGE/TENSION that is important, not the brand of yarn.
For your convenience, listed below are the specific yarn ranges used to create our photographed models.

Ribbed Shells Blanket
Mary Maxim's Baby Kashmere

Striped Cables Blanket
Mary Maxim's Baby's Best

Lovey Baby Blanket
Mary Maxim's Starlette

Cables Go Round Blanket
Mary Maxim's Baby Kashmere

Rainbow Entrelac Blanket
Mary Maxim's Prism

Sweetheart Lace Blanket
Mary Maxim's Twinkle

Double Hearts Blanket
Mary Maxim's Baby's Best

Little Blossoms Baby Blanket
Mary Maxim's Baby's Best

Garter & Slip Stitch Blanket
Mary Maxim's Baby's Best